T0334932

Somebody Stand Up and Sing

Hugh Seidman

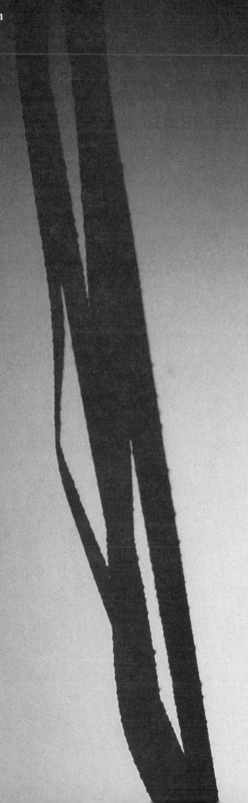

New Issues Poetry & Prose

A Green Rose Book

New Issues Poetry & Prose
The College of Arts and Sciences
Western Michigan University
Kalamazoo, Michigan 49008

First Edition, 2005.

ISBN   1-930974-52-3 (hardbound)
              1-930974-53-1 (paperbound)

Library of Congress Cataloging-in-Publication Data:
Seidman, Hugh
Somebody Stand Up and Sing/Hugh Seidman
Library of Congress Control Number: 2004116690

Editors   Herbert Scott, Lisa Lishman
Designer   Mary Pat Nickels
Art Director   Tricia Hennessy
Production Manager   Paul Sizer
                     The Design Center, Department of Art
                     College of Fine Arts
                     Western Michigan University

Somebody Stand Up and Sing

Hugh Seidman

New Issues

 WESTERN MICHIGAN UNIVERSITY

Also by Hugh Seidman

Collections:
Collecting Evidence
Blood Lord
Throne/Falcon/Eye
People Live, They Have Lives
Selected Poems: 1965-1995

Chapbooks:
12 Views of Freetown, 1 View of Bumbuna

Anthologies edited by Hugh Seidman:
Equal Time (Co-edited with Frances Whyatt)
Westbeth Poets (Co-edited with Richard Zarro)

For three estimable men:

Kaicho *(Grandmaster) Tadashi Nakamura, 9th Dan*
Founder: Seido Karate

Jorge Stolkiner, M.D.
Founder: Open Orgonomy

M. Ziesk, Master Optician

neither yellow bile of hatred
nor the scarlet of fame
nor green of hope

> —*Zbigniew Herbert*
> "Mr. Cogito's Heraldic Meditations"

Hearing the immense call of the Particular, despite the
earthly law that sentences memory to extinction.

> —*Czesław Miłosz*
> "Capri"

Now to Tumbez
In manly power.

Men buy a whorehouse
For a barrel of flour.

Whiskey gone;
Six-quid advance.

High time:
To stand up and dance.

> —Variation on "Blow Ye Winds"

Contents

IV. 2 Songs

V.

I.

Gail

I am sixteen you are my first love.
Your breasts are small under yellow cashmere.

The plastic surgeon has smoothed your cheerleader nose.

It is Sunday at your uncle's in Borough Park in Brooklyn.
The light of the heavens whitens the floor.

I am kissing you in the taste of cigarette, the odor of perfume.

I am sixteen and do not know
that I will never not remember this afternoon.

I am sixteen and do not contemplate
how envy corrodes friendship
how rage scars love
how failure tortures arrogance.

I am sixteen and do not recall
each interred under the blanched floor.

I am sixteen and do not imagine
how you are each who turns away
how you are each from whom I will turn.

I am sixteen and can think of nothing
but the pungency of cigarette, the reek of perfume.

As you lean back in the smoke that swirls about your face.

On the Other Side of the Poem

1

The April rain has a smell
that lingers upon grass and earth

and the diffused gray of the city sky
makes the car lights more luminous

this might be a fantasy but it is rather the other side of the poem

on the other side of the poem
I see a form in the shadows:
legs, a breast, an obscured face

and some who no longer pace Earth

on the other side of the poem
I am writing the poem
in their immense silence

of grief without reference

each dawn on the other side of the poem
comets streak the sky

permission is asked to enter the abstractions
infecting syllables

when we cannot find the counters
to clarify the emotion that engulfs us

I am often speaking of this
with someone in my head
who is never absent

on the other side of the poem

2

Now the stunning sun shines
on the other side of the poem

objects of an age: condom, cigarette, microchip

ten or a hundred or a thousand years ago
it was said saints walked among the people

on the other side of the poem
is the blank world past which there is nothing

and the other world
of endless possibility

which are the same worlds
in so far as memory and imagination converge in the actual

though sometimes
I forget who walks the rooms

if I am the son or the father
with a woman or with Mother

while the mausoleums of the clouds
disperse and gather

while the vaults of the oceans are rebuilt and leveled

the clamor of the armies and of the engines
that Alexander brought to Phoenicia to raze Tyre

we are born to Earth
and made its rulers

until each is the mortal alien
stranded without choice on earth

in whose gravity
the mourner kneels

on the other side of the poem

Case History: Melancholia

In 1965
I enrolled in the psych ward at Mt. Sinai.

I read the *Cantos* with the *Annotated Index*.
The famous poetess visited me
before she was famous.

They assigned me
the pretty nurse
from the plains of Kansas—
to coax truth from my lips.

Her hair was corn silk.
Her eyes were blue discs.

But I would not talk
would not take meds,
though on Broadway the Tofranil-Ritalin-Artane-Mellaril cocktail
used to upraise me
for an hour
before it crashed me,
out of phase.

It does not cohere, Pound said.
How write the epic
if the heroes were dead?

Years later, watching TV, it dawned:
it need not—cohere—
though others had been there before me.

Discharged,
I walked Broadway again,
starting equal.

Though personally,
I hardly care anymore.

Let the Muse keep the work
if she wants to,
poor woman.

Postpartum depressed,
bleary with Alzheimer's,
enduring our imprecations
no less than the dead who flutter around us more and more.

For now the starts of stories begin to serve ends,
and we see who rises or falls.

Do I go off here? where it is neither of Heaven,
nor of God.

Nor of 20 more IQ points.

Autobiography

Just half-century Brooklyn,
a Catskill comic's revel,
the onion-and-poppy rolls
on Ratners' tables.

Not, God forbid:
famine, plague, or flood;
poverty, war, torture,
or whatever genius of evil.

I had just woken up
to infinity and zero
to the clock and the ruler
to the rage of onanism.

Rock 'n' roll tumult,
against Mater and Pater,
mouthing "Heartbreak Hotel"
to Barbara's fired lips.

Or first-rhymed tongues:
a Jewish princess like a nun,
a sheer-bloused Gentile
intoning the Bible.

Under God the sun
forgive the pun
shtik infects the blood
though it's anyone's fiction.

Heaven knows why
yet how absurd
for a mathematician
to be tuned to words.

Leaden as the Sheepshead sinkers
the day I hooked
the biggest cod
that would have won the pool.

Had I not been the boy
to whom the captain gave
a chit to sail free
that I never used.

Palms and Hands

Larry shrugged,
jerked up his palms
to mimic a certain dictator:
"I take no part.
I love everyone.
Do not involve me."

But Bill shoved out his palms
like his mechanic father
(with cuts and grease):
"Don't let these be yours."

Unknown, of course,
to Lydia and Paul
young, obscure,
quoting Keats
on their magazine
Living Hand:
"warm and capable
. . . see here it is—
I hold it towards you."

Invoking monkey
mouth, eyes, and ears
shut with palms;
or *His* nailed palms;
or "Hands up!"
as the Saturday matinee
cowboy or soldier
lifted his life-lined,
creased palms.

Whereas Riva
rested her shorn
skull in her palms
(her German lover
dead in Nevers)

and someone raised
the knuckles of his splayed hand
to his eyes, walking
backwards out on
Hiroshima Mon Amour
against the concussion
of the shock wave
of the firestorm.

I Do Not Know Myself

I do not know myself
I go to dark and am of dark

Ignorant of myself

I sleep and dream—
But not enlightened

Nor when I wake
And remember dream

All I have not seen
All I will not see again

That I will take to ignorant dark

Desire is unchanged
Year on year it is on

Each page to turn
Each face to love

If I lived
Till the end of the world

It would never be done

Once I was a son
Once I had all the time in the world

Now a day starts
Now it ends
Now a window is dark

The Streetlight

Gathers the silence into itself
so that it may shine in a little while.

Whose twilight is this?
lights coming on.

I was born and I die in the present.
The sky is pallid blue.

Another year enters my life in the present.
Another year in the present of silence.

Each little window
radiates, in the present.

I was given my life and no other.
I was given a present and no more.

Opened to the epiphanies
of the withheld breast of the past in the present.

There are solitary guides, who guide me,
in the present.

The white bear that scents
the unseen seal on the pack ice.

The black bear that stalks the rapids for the salmon
come 4,000 miles to be reborn.

Circling the sun of the now,
in the night of the present.

The streetlight aura glows
yellow against the sky.

The streetlight burns,
until the sun quenches it.

The *Daily Racing Form*

On my last day at the *DRF*,
Aman, the Iranian manager,
celebrated with sandwiches.

I had tech-written data control
for Phoenix and Lexington.

I had documented source code
to parse a half-million horses.

Until then none knew I "wrote."

And Taiwanese Robert confessed:
he preferred programs to people,
since computers are dependable.

And Sean from Beijing lamented:
only the rich had time for poems,
how great to do what you wanted.

And Aman spoke fluent English,
but did not "feel" English poems.

And his daughter read Persian,
but algebraic Khayyám "lost" her.

And Aman corrected my stressing
of *Rubáiyat,* whose quatrains, he said,
are like quadratic equations.

And Rumi, he said, had said
that we are pieces of God.

And so, on my last day, I learned poetics.

As on each day, to and from work,
the train light on the white wall tiles
had taught me briefly of the light.

How each might face transcendence.

Hudson

unwavering noon, self-minus
sun flake on the levels of gold

there are names for these things: rose, brick, plate glass

the annunciation of the sparrow
a gene for anxiety

add hope, fear, greed, desire

no rest but the shade
to which a sun implodes

perhaps on other worlds others walk streets
muse on the weather

psyches built, say, on a double sun of unwavering noon

the balm of such congruence

•

thick, white, stick bicyclists painted on the esplanade to Chambers

glinting Jersey cars
helicopter blades under a ledge of cloud

alien first descent past the Trade Towers
drifting in on the flyway to LaGuardia

landscape, local, locale: the man-made made man

trying to open to something like days' unraveling waves

•

blue pulled toward fire out toward the skyscraper lights

ancient mausoleums
upheavals from personal terror

dark pier jut into dark water

turquoise, indigo, aqua, lapis; under the molten, under the bruise of
night

blood in your lips
as a man I violated the boundary of your mouth

I say this because in the phantasmagoria
I was woman and man

in another story you turn men to stone

though here, out of narrative, poignant at Morton Street against the
twilight

•

incomprehensible rain under sun

heap-leach haze-gold fused to evening
water's green-gray dense pliance

shadowed face bent to the shadows to drink and be salvaged

tiered buildings like Titanics
yellow truck-trailer's anonymous corpse conjoined to the
numberless

a boy swept from the rocks at the Verrazano stanchion
tomb cold draining past Liberty

it need not cohere but how could it not?
without context, for which all are accountable

this is for you of the future: one was here who is gone, into the
eigen levels

II.

2 Poems

Sit-In: Columbia University—'68

Spring, thus renewal,
amid strike and transformation.

While the subjugators
of riot and insurrection
in jackboots and helmets
twirled billies or rapped trees.

Though hardly Warsaw,
or Jerusalem of the skulls
impaled by the Assyrians,
or Tyre sacked by Alexander.

But the arrested and freed,
though bystanders
clubbed later, as occurs,
went unmarked in the news.

Famine: Biafra—'70, Sudan—'98

In the basement to recycle
a neighbor wisecracks
as if I have felled
the newsprint trees.

But there the four-color,
front-page child stares,
as it had in black and white,
as I read what I had read.

And upstairs in the dark,
palms shut eyes unto dark.

As when the body, enraged,
lies down, though alive:
helpless before Earth,
impotent to disinter the sun.

7 Times Down — 8 Times Up

Did I not think of the beautiful elsewhere?

On any night
did I not live in rooms of the mind?

Block on block of apartments,
people in bars.

How many times
did I ride the subway?

How many days
did I shop for clothes?

I shall mourn for no reason.
I shall fear for myself.

I shall read of a famous Buddhist
and vow compassion.

A contradiction in terms.

I shall kneel in the dark,
with what place to turn?

I shall make the face in the mirror
I have not learned.

Vexilla Regis Prodeunt Inferni

tunnel air-purification monolith
viscid sun: stasis, uproar
iced-Absolut space amid minor chords

black, abandoned ferry-terminal maw
luminous cloud edge, gold-mirror water
kayak's dark, fluttering oar

ocherous taint, engorged orange
wind heat of Bessemer heavens
sky as of a pyre under horizon

white yacht on fractaled ultramarine
two mottled, brown mallards
parallel, between piers, to shore

garish, neon Travelers red umbrella
diamond Venus pressured in carbon blue
lit high rises like computer boards

undulating, gleaming wave scales
souls flicked from a cigarette
to rise into the inverted firmament

Oracles

Cassandra: West Street, Dusk

Fingers count.
Recount portents.

Bottles and cans.
Two store carts.

Homeless throne.
"Hour of Judgment!"

River barrier.
No metamorphosis.

Nail-head sun.
Placental blue.

Current fate.
None doubts her.

Throne: folded.
Carts: pulled.

Tiresias: 6th Avenue, New World Coffee

Bearded—wields cane, mutters.
Counterwoman cedes comp cup.

(Against violence?
From guilt?
For charity?)

Grimaces to his back.
But, for the fluke witness—what act?

Or—hunchback.
Shopping cart, sandals, socks.

Badgers the male barista.

(Scorns her?
Quits distraught?
Offers the cash register?
Hugs Mother?)

Sky-honed buildings.
Young, old—roused past plate glass.

Whirls, rivets witness eye: "Onward!"

Red, Red

I was dreaming you on TV
between fiction and news.

A doll: tiny pearls
sown to your underwear.

Yet alive, your tongue
at red-mouthed song.

I was ashamed to touch
the cleft between your legs.

In a house, with the trunk
from my boyhood room.

And Mr. Bear: not stuffed,
but a walker and a talker.

The other dolls:
somehow broken, yet whole.

So that I cried: *how cruel,*
but Mr. Bear went on.

Before the frizzy-haired:
not you, but your doubles.

And the rooms: myself,
as I was or as I might be.

The sun: inching
north to zero, like infection.

As when the child
sweats with no milk.

Before the fervid, dazzling
remnant of Mother.

And Mr. Bear: unto granite,
what never yields.

And the electric-haired:
the sexual wire—red, red.

I Could Not Say

I could not say I had averted Brooklyn:
envy, cruelty, treachery, rage, hatred.

I could not say I had forsworn vengeance:
broken nose, tooth—for broken nose, tooth.

I could not say I had avowed the good:
remorse, empathy, loyalty, mercy, love.

I could not say I had quit the stoop:
Jew Ganz, my hero, wrestling bully Joey.

I could not say I had settled truth:
scraped knee, filthy hand, football, punchball.

In spring my father took me to the field
where batters smacked the balls.

At camp: trapped Cassiopeia; belted Orion;
Venus the false star, even then.

As there God oversaw the cohorts
tightening the tefillin like tourniquets.

Recompense

The employed worked,
but the subway "poor"
(said by the non-poor)
shuttling where?

Circle of wheel shriek,
but had these sinned?

Some in suit or dress:
not rich, not poor?

The headhunter ordered:
Pfizer needs writers.
Ignore the carpentry.

Thus, I testified,
at nail and Spackle,
for dollars per hour,
to be called if hired.

So at the third rail
mice again scuttled;
loudspeakers garbled:
track, shuttle.

I took my seat
(that is never ours)
to go as I had come.

To weigh who deserved
worldly, earned bread.

At Times Square the sun:
like the chord
struck in *Barabbas*
when he climbs from
the sulfur mine.

A proffered hand
begged my quarter.

Someone, as ever,
tendered less or more.

Like the swapped one,
like the hammered one.

Red Thread

What is the news to me?
I can only write the one poem.

Jukebox bourbon 40 years ago,
making sundown.

Lust for transcendence, oblivion.
Words built to anything.

Anything built in words in the mind.
Where do I find such nonsense?

Here is a version:
"Judge the witness. Blame the messenger."

Here is a girl: sold as a whore
via poverty and AIDS.

If not her, here is a girl:
sold as a whore via poverty and AIDS.

Song that thinks, dreams us,
sounding nowhere but to the self.

I can hear it now under the bourbon,
sun gone down.

New hundred-dollar bill,
incorporating Reich's "red thread."

Religious

Mind-numbing work came to mind, walking to work,
to document FoxPro at the *Daily Racing Form*

Though surely one would not compare that, say,
to Carnegie's puddlers on the steel-making floor
at 12-hour days in '85 for 15 cents an hour.

Those who might have referenced something of the body.

As thus, also, did *subtle thought* spring to mind,
as of someone who must have lived long ago.

Tiring, say, not in body or in mind—down millennia.

Macy's Elegy

Once—my delusional father.

His "oracle" had ordered:
scrap the gray coat; get the brown coat.

I could not help him on the buy-and-sell floor.

Now—the gourmet fast food:
pesto asparagus, penne, sun-dried tomatoes.

A man and son eating salmon.

Masonic ring like my father's:
compass, right-angled ruler—encircling a diamond.

Brother in the fraternity of Father.
Anonymous, infinite as one.

Thwarting hunger, slaking thirst.

As the adepts teach: *praise where you are.*

Genre

topless, who hates
herself, who feels

powerful, dancing
for men, older

cop who guards her—
resolved after

failed love, the slaughtered
innocent—how long

to forgive him, how . . . ,
but this is genre:

cop and whore—
poet, ingénue

he left New York
but did not take her—

years and years:
fingering her

key-ring, steel,
cigar-cutter

gift—secret,
yet of each fact,

as lived by each,
as if any were of one

drama, acting
the arbitrated

script—the plots
stop, the film

reels on: hope
and dream, genre

High School

Enamored of Euclid's circles and squares.

Van Doren's *World Poetry:*
orated to brainy, Episcopal Judith.

Or rhymed hot "God" and "love,"
useless as seduction.

Slip straps under a sheer blouse.
Screwing the college boyfriend.

(Did I care? Knowledge was power?)

Though in English Miss H. alleged:
I "stole" Bradbury, Salinger.

(Her techie? Not a wordsmith?
Text: "Why Pity Adults?")

Alone, intoned my people's long lines,
precursing Whitman.

Read Bell's mathematical *Men.*

Daydreamed torrid lips of Judith—
yet unkissed? before pure number.

Artist Whom I Wed in New York

Scrapbook, barefoot girl (1874).

Right arm: basket;
right hand: pitcher;
left hand: cow browsing hay.

Sky, tree, thatched roof, geese.

Bonnet; long skirt;
half-sleeved, collarless shirt
buttoned to the neck.

Jayne rode Indiana ponies.
Her Dunkards fled Europe (1719).

Inveighers against:
worldly act & dress.

Jayne: almost lithograph,
but for Christ knows what.

Consecrated to canvas.

Housewife ads, women drivers,
quilts, witch tortures.

Grandparents' cerulean,
campground-slide sky.

Nancy Drew sleuthing:
iconic Rushmore, Old
Faithful, Grand Canyon.

Volunteer Templar
of His sheltered homeless.

Leather-booted/-jacketed:
retempered unto
His pacifist, Mennonite wrath.

Zealot of hue, hymn (2004);
of Memling's irenic faces.

Dearest Jayne: brushing
graying, straight hair
in the steel megalopolis.

Light of the World

8:40 A.M.: Christopher down Bedford to Sixth.
The light of the world shines.

That is, a floodlight burns spectacularly in the gray light.

Someone films something that needs this light.
Until the frames rot, until the last image passes.

Aunt Florence will not see this, cancerous in Brooklyn.
Youngest of Grandmother Rose.

Whose Anne died of endocarditis, before penicillin.
Whose Nat went four months before his brother, my father.

A vector pointing at me has ended in me.

Gray light where the light of the world shines.
Making day day.

Ally, Enemy

On Nardil, thought:
what, unthought,
bled thoughts?

On Nardil, dozed:
images flared, went.
How hold event?

Sipped coffee to keep up.
One came in dark.
Ally, enemy.

Mother tongue
forbidding play
in streets minus her.

Had birth shrieks
depressed her?
loosed paranoia?

But why repeat
what she mouthed
to any ear?

Three-year-old's bed
in parents' room.
He did not talk.

But for how long?
Stubborn son's
art to thwart her?

Words withheld
revenging what?
Mad idea.

Or—just the famed
gold hoard
of Midas turds?

Though, as heard:
*I learned speech
at her knee.*

Mirrored left eye
keeps her alive:
in contact, kind.

But no kiss: dead, buried—
just what is.
Ally, enemy.

On Nardil, dreamt:
a tree split cement—
bare, gnarled.

On Nardil, slept:
roots twined, dug—
touched her head.

Somebody Stand Up and Sing

Today, the computer headhunter, as I have said.

Buzzed on Starbucks' house blend among the brokers.

More and more: Father in the mirror (for better commerce?).

Yesterday, masked revelers outside a building.
Imagine, unlimited identity.

No match for the laureates, I know—still, word opens.

> One night, one day.
> Weight into volume.
>
> Or is it:
> volume into weight?
>
> Herbert's line?:
> *absolute ear*
> *versus immense range.*

Or perhaps the marbled-library lecture.

It appears (one infers?)
Auden felt guilt like Vallejo's:

> *Someone passes by counting with his fingers.*
> *How speak of the not-i without screaming.*

Yes, caffeine edge.

Eyes open to piped-in guitar.
Something as if *ancient.*

Father's paradoxical neck cords in my too-tight white shirt.
Should not the corpse be getting thinner?

Suddenly, a woman's laugh:
like a backbone of pain,
like a child's duty never learned.

Vibrations of sound to dark, to light, to ever-widening dark.

So that I say,
as to anyone,
but to myself:
"Somebody stand up and sing."

III.

Seasonal

February

Jet glint over Newark,
false-spring twilight.

Cops kick a man in the cold
as we pay for bread.

Unborn shadows want light.
Unfed cat: *me now, me now.*

August

Three subway Peruvians:
pipe, strum, drum.

We clap and drop tribute—
till muffled by the express.

A man supplicates for change.
On or off—open-and-shut.

November

Black pearls, white pearls.
Winston's gold jubilee

at Met's oils and marbles.
Jet-blue-haired, red-faced

Chief Red Jacket glares
on the Stanhope matches.

New Years

Nomad starves, cripple hobbles,
celebrity yields charity.

Good leg limps?
Full stomach hungers?

Electric apple falls.
Broadway fireworks stutter.

2 Poems

L.A.

Pool sun.
Cool rum.

Some fun.
Rental car.

Miles from
riot shots.

Awry AC.
Hot one.

Alms

Salt, sugar.
Right, left.

West, east.
Profit, debt.

Vice versa.
Vis-à-vis.

One: for hand.
Two: for eyes.

Filthy Lucre

Sale

Clerk: "A year's pay in
Brazil." Leather-coat-tag brag:
Scars make skins unique.

Saint-Gaudens

Thumb and fingers to
rub off Liberty's gold dress,
and the eagle's wing.

7000 at $16^{1/2}$

VP OKs dad's
3 jobs' pay stubs. Frilled, tickled
daughter squirms, giggles.

Bright Spring

Astaire in *Carefree*.
1973, with
E. A simpler world.

Was it? CNBC quotes.
Black and white till lead is gold.

Hatted Army

Boys' head-
stone Hebrew
capping men.

5 Poems

For Harvey Shapiro

5 P.M. Often
rain, thunder. More CO_2?
"No," your view, "God's wrath."

•

Summer's starved-bluefish,
sea-churn silver. Winter's birth-
day, cake-sugar dust.

For M. Ziesk

Ounce pain, till temples'
balanced pressure. Jarred frames show:
past, past; rebalance.

For C.

Film-star daughter. Same
face bones; black hair, not white-blonde.
How dark a sun chars.

For Michael Heller

Krishna's dolls: babe to
bones. Beast axing a man-faced
cow: *thoughts' death—and death:*

thought champagne kills. Glass at
lips—though nova out Earth.

For David Ignatow

Some gut fish; cut boards,
breathe sawdust. Some chart stars. So
far—who catches them?

Indented
nip-

ple, thin
arm,

unmarred
palm

on
hip, am-

ple
hair, or

lain down:
un-

appeasable
future.

3 Poems

Malibu, 1976

Tan, bared to water:
courtesan, carnal laughter.
Crossing youth's country

toward the Hereafter.
O muse of that capital!

Tryst

Wheel jerked against rage
braking as we slide past rage—
spun, stunned, horn raging.

2.19.85

Ear on the pillow.
My own heart. Dusk. Dawn. Only
now—but to forget.

Ingot in the fire. And you
are almost here—forged from dark.

A to Z

First memory: black mutt's tiny-teeth bite.
Eighth birthday snubbed by raven Helen.

First-grade "bad" stool under Hubbard's desk.
Jail promised to the yeller of "stinker."

East 8th's stickballers: sewer to sewer.
New "fag" piano mocked by those Olympians.

Mother's quarters filched for sports cards:
flipped heads/tails, volatile as futures.

School files for cops, banks, bosses.
Marked by wrinkled Jeffries, Milhard, Russo.

Stamps, models, microscope, chess.
Yo-yos, marbles—spring of the cosmos.

Bakelite, rouge-buffed, black dodecahedron:
lost, unsorted, untransformed, nonorderable.

Mother: Nursing Home

Coney Island

Paper-thin wrist skin.
Nurse combs: "SUUU!san." Grins, save her
hard eye. Sun. Son. Goes,

comes. Unrecognized?
None, unkind.

POA

I make her sign. Last
ticket. Some built pyramids.
She goes with them. None

knows her triumphal
chicken scratch

Pneumonia

60 in winter.
AC, heat on. "It's Hugh." Eyes
raise. Astronaut. Strapped

in: oxygen-masked,
flight-suited.

Testament

"I gave my life for
you." Blame? No. Means: she would yet.
Now, my wife: undressed.

Bequest, splendrous, from
her mercy.

Father Dreams

Topcoated mourners
in fedoras. You, in white
pajamas. Nineteen-six.
Son again with Mother.

•

Boat rocked us closer
than ever. You considered
immutable stone: one-
by-two-foot water slab.

•

Waxed limousine; torn,
black ribbon. My/your belly
curve. Hands washed at the door.
Broken, hearted chamber.

Father Soul

Knickerbocker Bar — 1990

Prattled, peed, proudly
swiped napkins. Indeed, suits' wads:
snot, sweat, tears, blood, phlegm.

Liberty Street — 1925

Built radios, wired
Waldorf's phones. TV, PC:
Father soul bathes me.

Composition: 7 Poems

T. Rex

Unearthed dwarfing men.
60 million years.
Up/downwind.

Oath

I swear: I am the
executor of
Mother's will.

Past Happiness

One must go to Hell.
I know, I know. Head
does but won't.

Ambition

To be no one. Not
only Son to check-
mate Father.

Wail

Newborn's mere hunger,
but "mere"? History:
just lament?

Library

Eros unlocked. No-
thing lovelier than
"demotic."

Capital

The Ironclads! Backed!
Full faith/credit of
Parnassus!

Composition: Voice of Our Time

Genius incalculable.
Us: chip, chip, chip.

Buy Ultra at 12,
which is the sweat of men.

Put in the kitchen sink.
Work X hours a week.

Father, competitor.
Mother, rejecter.

Do others cross fingers?
Else, erect the day.

6 P.M. and just started,
and so many to feed.

Composition: 2 Poems

1

Each day—synopses,
reviews, plots. You might ask: who
cares? Coat-pocket stone.

"O" mouth—under clouds.
Adrift, as from a perfume
ad; or, sipping all

planet tears. No more
yells in her head—far, closer.

2

Type, send—gone. Hundred-
year-old "Negress": blue-jean quilts,
hooked rugs from nylons.

Third-world Vermeer: paint
on newsprint scraps, matchboxes.
Sly Emily, mad

Vincent, weird Henry's
comic-strip hermaphrodites.

Composition: 3 Poems

Poem Vs. Stock

Monday. Good for what?
Scavenging news: *Poor child*
fed . . . rice, water. All

eat?—if words choose? No myths.
Youth ends. Have no intention?

Google

So much talk when cut
is task. *N* billion sites
passed so fast. Words what

but past? Sent, saved, archived,
cataloged draft—fame at last!

It Can't Matter Now

Rub out who wrote. Rain
on rock. Rebirth. Wound, with
context. *Shoe,* say, found

in streets. Loss? Glut? Waste? Ruin?
Immortals' memorial.

Found Poem: Microloans

Fifty dollars is a fortune
Nations flout women.
Banks scorn mothers.
Usurers steal capital.

Nations flout women.
Poverty lacks collateral.
Usurers steal capital.
Hoping is dependence.

Poverty lacks collateral.
A woman fears risk.
Hoping is dependence.
Microloans lift women.

A woman fears risk.
Mothers feed families.
Microloans lift women.
Women form groups.

Mothers feed families.
How do I contribute?
Women form groups.
A group backs payback.

How do I contribute?
A woman wove cloth.
A group backs payback.
A woman sold bread.

A woman wove cloth.
A woman fired bricks.
A woman sold bread.
No mouth is exempt.

A woman fired bricks.
Children sicken.
No mouth is exempt.
One-fifth of Earth starves.

Children sicken.
Banks scorn mothers.
One-fifth of Earth starves.
Fifty dollars is a fortune.

Joan

I didn't know I'd
long for Joan. Fall, once before:
silver teardrop with

a diamond on a gold
chain—nude, in a Polaroid.

•

Sea rage past rain. "Give
your *heart* to the wave." Dumb word.
Never assuaged? A

girl, burned. Belief, with a sword,
in steel—like desire in Joan.

•

No time like the past
for the present. No time to
mine the silver tears.

Days go. Nothing stills the wind.
Diamond heart cleaved by Joan.

IV. 2 Songs

200 in Hell

200 in Hell
Where our sweat is predictable

The part of ourselves
Still marred by the mortal

Sometimes the devil
Guns his convertible

He looks like a hunk from *Gentleman's Quarterly*
With the pageboy black curls
And the six-pack abdominals

But at times he must say
What the hell!
And drop the charade

With the hooves and the horns
And the big red boner
And the tail and the smoke
Blowing out of his nose

I think it slaps us to the real for a while
Until he's gone
With a blonde
And we wonder if we saw him

Though it's easy to rage tears
And I don't mean to bring you down

Yet even in the pit
Your life is your own

Old Scratch told me so
He's not a bad guy
Once you know him

As once upon a time
However far a time was
He floored the red Cadillac
Beneath the soot and the brimstone

With the bumper torpedoes
And the chrome and the whitewalls
And the shark fins with the top down
Though up or down
He didn't mind

And he boomed: *Sin* and *Death* and *Purgation*
And of course *Damnation*

It was nuts I know
To cavil with Satan
Though it's what may befall you

But if you want to know why
I landed here
In fact I forget
Though the reason must be clear

And that's the execration
He explained as we rode

Though perhaps it's an error
As when he'll arrive
To glide me to blue sky
If that's where Heaven is

So be it I don't give a damn
Wherever I am
Wherever I've been
After all these years

So gape at the stars
Though there are none
And wind all the broken clocks

200 in Hell
200 in Hell
And what's the temperature of Paradise?

He said about 72
Give or take a degree

And the angels have halos
Just like in the paintings

And suntans as in the movies
And it's always V-day each day

And all is as it is in all of our dreams

So here I bid you well
Though Beelzebub fell
And we seethe down here with him

12 Views of Freetown, 1 View of Bumbuna

damn thing
make you blind
make you deaf
trying to hear

—Overheard on Bethune Street (NYC)

1

Sergeant Burnhouse
Captain Blood
(not their names)
slice and cripple
lead the rebels
from the capital
to teach the President
a lesson
in his fortress
in his fortress
above the graves

2

Day fails
past cries
to house and phone

Souls convene
in the fires

Judge Osiris
wields the scale

Victims heavy
victors few

Listen: he was
dismembered too

Polluted tears
what do eyes do?

Stand still here
don't move

3

At the end
of the hospital
there's a picture
in a room
its black
macadam
runs to the tomb
of the unseen
driver
there's a white
center line
and then it's not a road
but the face
of the abyss
and the white
line cuts
up and down
the universe
where galaxies turn
over the accursed

4

Another blue morning
on the shores
of sleep

Another grain lost
from the rice
some keep

Doubtless
in a future
Burnhouse
and *Blood*

Will deny
what ones
some will say
they were

Protesting
innocence:
we hurt none

5

eyes burned
hands prayed

i had
no hands

blood ran

as a
faucet
runs—

into the sun

6

One saw the rich man
tongue was an ember

Somehow
it took his head

Swearing the oath
of lust and rebellion

Blood diamonds
grind the sea
they go down
against the will

As in Freetown
the machete trilled—

What branch
bleeds sky?

What leaf
is wind
of leg and arm?

Aleatoric
no matter the harm

7

And who will embrace
the Angel when he comes?

His granite tears
and his wings of flame

His body graven
with the glyphs of dream

Our life is glass
we see to the end

Everests erupted from the ocean floor
iron boiling in the earthly core

8

Burnhouse and *Blood*
were my men

Likewise
the boy
in the hospital bed

Do you think I care
who wins?

On your knees
and say: *Amen*

I shut my eyes
and tears are stone

I cry for God
who is so alone

My wings unfurl
and a city burns

I am that
from which
none returns

9

I am Osiris
a corpse
implores
the ostrich
feather that
balances
the heart

Though one
not weighed
stabs his
own heart
with the blade
used on those
he abused

"Kill till
all give in
for no goal
but to win"

10

I am Isis
there is red on my dress
and on my hem

Not from pools
where my brother rules

Nor from laying
my womb
on his wounds

Nor from furnaces of incest

But gang-raped
shot in the face

Martyred
in the marble
of sodomy

How should I have pled?

11

Colonel Top Gorilla
Captain Burntrouble
(yes the comic
macabre
stand-ups)
lead the rough
at Bumbuna
damned versus
damned for
the dam
where Rokel
severs jungle
on the black
5,000 note
as decades
make no watts
whatever
one is worth

12

i believe
minus hands

when i touch
myself as man

i thirst
when i drink

Christ is salt
the sea
is blood

black arm
white stump

like the mad
on the ward

13

I am the Angel
I hear the tunes

Mourners wail
in endless rooms

Ice and star
and rage
are mine

Each held
is mine

I point my finger
I sign your name
I am the Angel
I turn the page

V.

Burial Garden Memorial: Father-in-Law

William Holsinger (1922-2001)

Son-in-law's Wordsworth's "Ode."
Granddaughter's clarinet "Rock of Ages."
Brethren brother's Armageddon eulogy.

Cabinet carpenter.
Newspaper deliverer.
Green bean sower.
Bendix brake assembler.
World War sailor.

One daughter's barn, field, I-80 horizon cars.
Prairie urn, sudden wind, dusk shade, immobile sun.
No hours but the conflagrated hour.

Venerated in his name.

Step stone, tomato plant, trumpet ivy, marigold.
Blue-glass-sphere sky/ground mirror.

Crow & Turtle

you were savoring your farm girlhood:

—swiped at the cabbage moth

—coaxed the stray, nosing lamb

—spat out the waxy milkweed sap

I was exalting past women:

—SoHo-bar, starlet-faced, art darling

—angelic, blonded, dance robot

—skeletal, micro-skirted, IRT anima

but a crow pecked a turtle

to which you bent, abruptly:

—for pity?

—to cut exult?

ourselves now, obdurate, wrenched, far back:

—pony: yelled at, shying from your hand

—teddy bear: shunned, cast from my bed

ergo, so that, then, for example:

—cat your father drowns

—toy, wood sword my mother cracks

green mountain, white church steeple

mown, shadowed path to the river, blasted with goldenrod

True Tunes

Rapunzel: Starbucks

Acquaintance's
acquaintance.

Once: young, tousled
blonde at a window.

Divorced, I heard.

Ex's third:
half her age.

First: an actual princess.

Any contract's:
cash, clout, position.

Shrink, M.D.—
grown kids, clients.

No ring—
coffee, a sandwich.

Giggles, like a girl,
at the register.

"I can't add."

Bites cake; flips
a psych journal.

Sudden ravaged face—
with normalcy.

Almost notices me.

Hercules

C on the elevator,
skirt up, unfaithful
to another.

S's nipple in the bar,
with soon-to-be-ex hubby
the famed painter.

J, the first time,
post lover, to see
if she *liked* it.

E's menstruating,
shaven, pristine
kid sister.

B, on the street,
picked up—luminous,
later, in the dark.

Stroller deranged
Mother deserts
where horses canter
the bridle path.

Matter's notorious
silence.

Desire blistering
this side of the sun.

Though hard
to recall details
or why labors.

Venus: 1 Train

Gold tiny heart locket.
Gold nostril ring.

Mauve toes, nails.
Red, cat-eye shades.

Earlobe diamond.
Platinum's black roots.

Taut, navel-pierced,
exposed belly.

Fuchsia, glossed lips.
Arm: butterfly tattoo.

Sighs, stirs—
what annoys her?

Profiled, fisted chin,
like *The Thinker.*

Virginal as when
she strode sea foam.

Though her tongue
will soon sap a boy.

That which hurts
or heals the world?

Strappy, wedge heels:
whose bonds?

Silver bracelets:
whose shackles?

Adored past
the masturbatory light.

O, immortal traveler,
yet your disciple.

Aurora

Poor thing,
nothing but vistas.

Prelude to dull,
whole days.

Weary of her
boring stories.

Lunch at hot spots
the dark shuts.

Why not quit her job?
or find one?

Say yes, no—
not get personal.

She'd like to scream,
just a little.

Be her slut sister—
the total show.

Lustrous, absolute,
irreducible silver.

Commerce: asleep
like a child.

Dusk: powdered,
eyelined, rouged.

But whether for
lust, love, languor.

After leather night:
still, yet, I fell.

Destined to wake
to familiars.

Drear, drab—dear!—
enkindled chill.

TECH TALES

Dr. Help

Houston pop rock over
Telescan user support.

Friday, midnight, EST.
This is for Mary from Joe.

Hope—from the American dark.
Huge as the Rockies.

It shoots the moon,
excretes malls and cars.

Till Dr. Help picks up:
does his job, rights wrong.

As always I thought:
get work, go on.

But what of Mary or Joe?—
mad, murderous, suicidal?

At the end of the lines
of listening and talking.

29th December 2000

PhoneFree.com:
Let freedom ring.

Venture startup:
Web calls for nothing.

At the pot-luck:
blinis to samosas.

"Model-thin" Jennifer,
like K so long ago.

Some want bucks?
or just to catch the show?

Before the weekend,
before the snow.

One for the road.
The 2 train home.

Everyone gone
to wherever they go.

Here's a joke:
we yawn and blow,
none the wiser.

Some crowed:
I made this—it's gold.

SETI

Some aim telescopes
to grab non-randomness.

Even if star travel
is relativistically
next to impossible.

Though some propose
n-spaces, warps, holes
to the heretofore remote.

Like those of Earth
trapped in this trope?

May instantiation not defile instance.

Omaha

Hotel TV:
Gere yet courts Roberts;
Nazis loft *die Blutfahne.*

Out back: frenetic,
unaware children.

Or—just one's own chaotic,
child breath.

"Defend the dead—
do not talk politics."

Elbows, street shouts:
a man smacking
his own face.

King said:
Christ's order,
Gandhi's tactic.

I do not mean we will not be ennobled,
borne home, says the Master to no one.

•

"Art cannot rival Hiroshima."

Hurtful past,
dread future.

Tears digitized to
"universal" English.

Raped, orphaned sisters
wrapped in *hijab.*

Archetypal
Protocols of Zion.

"Painstaking
human parts catalog."

We pass ignorantly:
create despair,
glimpse light.

"Rama,"
said the assassinated.

•

Here to earn my rate.

Like the squirrel:
tail fluttering,
acorns mouthed.

Hard-wired woe
potentiates sobering
moments of woe.

Noon runway.
Trance vengeance.

Rigid Iowa grid.

Lake Michigan
white wave.

Miles from Earth
clouds yoke Earth
to a universe.

Narrows Bridge.
Torch of Liberty.

Abrupt LaGuardia water.

"As if record were reason."

Joslyn

Workshop: Lorenzetti.
Last Communion St. Mary Magdalene.
Desert hermit fed by angels.
Her tears wet Christ's feet.
Dried by her hair.
Enrobes her: head to ankle.
Naked before a cave.

•

Di Credi.
Madonna & Child w/ Infant St. John & 2 Angels.
Daisies: Innocence.
Violets: Humility.
White roses: Purity.
Red roses: Martyrdom.
Far, separate, secular Florence.

•

Anonymous.
Mass St. Gregory.
Pope at the altar.
Candlestick, censer, vestment.
"Papal patrimony owed the poor."
Man-of-Sorrows' wounds.
Palm spurts chalice blood.

•

Workshop: Gossaert, a.k.a. Mabuse.
Madonna & Child w/ Sts. Catherine & Agnes.
Christ's brides.
No pagan wedlock.
"Word stops state not sword."
Catherine: broken torture wheel.
Agnes: reveals ring to lamb (God's).

•

Half-staff stars/bars.

Battery

Acrid, hosed, wrecking-ball rubble.
Bell Atlantic banner: "United We Stand."

North-End-and-Vesey snapshot tourists.

RESPIRATORS AND PROTECTIVE CLOTHING
REQUIRED IN THIS AREA

•

What acts for nation, cause, man/woman?

Backs bent hauling Pharaoh's blocks.

Noble wheel, temple, gun, space rocket?

•

Boarded-shut World Financial atrium.

Sun firewall guarding dark Ellis Island.

Cold wind at bare bench and shadow.

Dead-west Jersey's Exchange Place:
12-foot, back-skewered, bronze Polish officer.

"Katyn's thousands, Siberia's millions."

"Untitled"

South: conflagrant tower.
Foreground: rooftop observer.

Gray nebula spirals in hair—
yellow-red highlights, like fire.

Sunlit-brick shadow:
red-streaked, as of wounds.

Bluish-red shaded back,
like a flak jacket.

Gray-blue, chance, crowned visage
worms in smoke cabbage.

One roof: blue-black pit.
Two roofs: blue-white ice.

Pale-blue window; lit window.
Tiny, disparate.

•

Scrap falls—"People!"—"No!"—
yet yes, before, learned later.

Jayne's 2nd photo, not painted:
facial muscles bewailing.

Washington

Concrete slabs encircling the Monument.

America's one Leonardo, armed entrance guards.

True Colors: Meridian's 9-1-1 show.

Jayne's rendering: self as witness.

CBS interview: what had she hoped to say?

Georgetown opulence: coffee, fruit, scone.

Façade: "1796"; mild February.

Bronze-green *Freedom:* atop the Capitol.

Corot to Picasso: death year minus birth year.

Weight of faces: like the sand grains.

Anywhere: God's new/old magnitude.

Cherries' impending, memorial blossoms.

"Switch shut, circuit closed."

No time to explain before the street explodes.

New York

I read over my lines
(terrible hubris,
terrible debris).

I have been too soft:
car skid in the rain,
black eye over a woman,
105 fever of pneumonia.

I confess that my parents
suffered heart attack,
dementia, stroke.

Sometimes I had anger,
whatever it meant.

Sometimes I wept,
as if in spite of myself.

(Brown, thick smoke
against dusk turquoise.)

I had entered
fluorescent cubicles.

I had crossed tunnels
under tons of water,
under the tomb
that is cosmos.

I had poured coffee,
tasted bread,
watched TV
blaring stocks, war.

(The Airbus 300
has struck Belle Harbor.)

Fear is what I lacked
(terrible motion,
terrible implode),
down to the soles,
the involuntary wail
that changes soul.

Each atom of the body
from the start of the stars.

One molecule at least, say,
of Caesar's breath.

Oracle

YÜ — ENTHUSIASM

 CHÊN   AROUSING, THUNDER
K'UN   RECEPTIVE, EARTH

It furthers. Install helpers.
Set armies marching.

Beyond Description

Redreamed tabernacle.

"Particle by particle,
crystal by crystal."

History that divides and divides.

Weak, strong.
Weak, strong.

Unpitying history
erupted from dream.

•

Ruin in a time of ruin
to match the eulogies.

Temblors of "paradise."

Hubris of God
imposed on the actual.

Equality of
tragedy and revenge.

•

Dark drains from dark.

No way down from down:
afire, alight, aflame, ablaze with sun.

Holder's mistletoe dart
felled Balder.

Resurrected if all grieved.
Loki would not.

Indivisible "evil."

Gautama on the shore.
Commander where the river legions dwell.

Blue Suit, Gold Wing

Blue, wooly suit;
gold, wrist-braid
latitudes, longitudes.

Gold lapel wing,
breath in the cockpit—
I drop my bombs.

For I have trained,
little pants at knees,
shamed yet devoted.

Shopped, soap to scent,
to cosset her—
triumph of Mother.

Have zipped her
into blackest black—
to lure the coveted.

Learned her silences,
laws, judgments—
obedient chronicler.

Else, her rebuke:
father-spoilt face
of old, brittle photos.

I am her regent;
imperium's victor;
Pilate, transgressor.

Little bombardier,
verdict of birth—
blue suit, gold wing.

Engines thrum;
targets luminesce;
bunker busters glister.

Thinking of Warsaw

Simpler to throw a rock at an historical tank than to sift the rubble?
Simpler to sign the petition than to stand with some against others?

The sniper fires his rifle at his father's father's father's father's father.
Each night—as if impregnable—chain, dead bolt.

Some die who are silent, shamed.
Some die who will not change.

Sometimes, as if anew, I learn greed.
Nursing-home doctor cuts good eyes, bills Medicaid for cataracts.

Mengele needled dye into twins' eyes.
I need to assert that they are of sacred memory, not abstract.

Torturers pray, despots philosophize—all in the work of days.
Beria judged his victims "hardened, uncompromising."

For years, Mother fed from a stomach tube.
Outside: sea, gases, galaxies, radiation, darkness, interstellar dust.

•

Simpler for X to kill than not?
The pardoner shall not pardon.

Facts almost exceeding reckoning.
Wheel-chaired torso minus legs and arms.

Some immolate themselves and/or others.
Death unmeasured by life.

Mind and form of the beloved.
Though I swear that the atoms do not care.

Sometimes: the rage that could tear steel.
Sometimes: the small deliverance of sweat.

To push up from the floor on knuckles.
Portion of breath, its sustenance.

X = Y; evade the juggernauts?
No reprieve; write: tree, bird, flower, warlord.

Thinking of Baghdad

Flesh gorging on oxygen.
Apes of smoke and debris writhing and struggling in air.

Wails of the *infidels* and *assassins*.
Mutilations from the centuries of bronze.

I wanted to exonerate the infants.
The event horizon was white hot.

The infernos were igniting the armor between myself and the infants.
The projectiles were piercing the armor between myself and the infants.

•

There, city, just past imploded brick.
There, city, just past the trope for black holes.

Here, I resented the price of a loaf of bread.
Here, I sat on a park bench in the sun.

Here, I dozed—numb, livid (nine hours from bombs).
Here, I paid tax—to forge the uranium tanks.

Here, I tongued language.
Here, I pled: country! country! country!

•

It is good to be made naïve.
It is good that blood forces in gut, as in brain.

Dreams bloom to the chroma of terror.
Long ago I swore to uphold the *imperial power* of dream.

Shrapnel purifies the eye of the testifier.
Protozoa bore harder into the fly.

The warplane graphic rotates slowly on the vengeful news channel.
Fate reiterates: thirst, starve, curse, scream, burn.

Notes

1. Page 21: *eigen* levels

In Chapter 3 it was pointed out that the time-independent Schrödinger equation,

$$Hu(r) = Eu(r), \qquad\qquad (4.30)$$

is of the form known as an *eigenvalue equation*. . . . [The] eigenvalue equation thus states that an operator [H], acting on a function [$u(r)$], reproduces the same function multiplied by a constant factor [a number E, called the *eigenvalue*]. The function [that] satisfies the equation is called the *eigenfunction* of the equation corresponding to the particular corresponding eigenvalue. Note that in Eq. (4.30), the eigenvalue is the energy of the particle.
  —Robert H. Dicke and James P. Wittke, *Introduction to Quantum Mechanics* (Reading, Massachusetts, U.S.A. and London, England: Addison-Wesley Publishing Company, Inc., 1961), 69.

2. Page 26: *7 Times Down—8 Times Up*

Nana Korobi Ya Oki (If you fall down seven times, get up eight times). This is the most famous expression of Daruma Daishi, who was the first person to come from India and establish Zen in China.
  —Tadashi Nakamura (9th Dan), *Karate: Technique and Spirit* (Tokyo: Shufunotomo Co., Ltd., 1986), 161.

3. Page 27: *Vexilla Regis Prodeunt Inferni*

The banners of the King of Hell advance.
  —Dante Alighieri, *The Divine Comedy: Inferno*, trans. John D. Sinclair (New York: Oxford University Press, 1968), 420, 426.

4. Page 35: "red thread"

The social façade contains one (sometimes more) basic character trait as its means of meeting the environment. . . . It becomes the main character defense. Reich calls this trait the *red thread* and it must be recognized to understand and evaluate the individual. The basic character trait is never dissolved but remains always an integral part of the personality, although it may be modified. It may be socially acceptable—kindness, modesty, reserve, shyness, correctness, righteousness; or socially unacceptable—dishonesty, cunning, cheating.
  —Elsworth F. Baker, M.D., *Man in the Trap* (New York: The Macmillan Co.; London: Collier-Macmillan, Ltd.; 1967), 62–63.

Acknowledgments

The author thanks the following publications for first printing or, in one case, posting the indicated poems—some in a different form and/or with a different title.

12 Views of Freetown, 1 View of Bumbuna (Chapbook): "7000 at 16½ ," "Ambition," "Bright Spring," "Composition: Voice of Our Time," "Google," "It Can't Matter Now," and "Poem Vs. Stock"

Brooklyn Rail: "Aurora," "Hercules," and "Venus: 1 Train"

David Ignatow: An Anthology: "For David Ignatow"

Hamilton Stone Review (www.hamiltonstone.org): "Composition: 2 Poems" and "Burial Garden Memorial: Father-in-Law"

Hanging Loose: "Alms" and "Tiresias: 6th Avenue, New World Coffee"

Hotel Amerika: "Tech Tales"

House Organ: "18," "7 Times Down—8 Times Up," "Genre," "Hatted Army," "LA," "Malibu, 1976," "Sale," "Cassandra: West Street, Dusk," "Red, Red," "Red Thread," and "T. Rex"

Ironwood: "Saint-Gaudens"

My Business Is Circumference: Poets on Influence and Mastery: "200 in Hell"

Object: "Capital," "Library," and "Wail"

Paper Air: "2.19.85," "Past Happiness," and "Tryst"

Pequod: "Artist Whom I Wed in New York," "Found Poem: Microloans," "Thinking of Baghdad," and "Thinking of Warsaw"

Poetry: "Hudson," "I Do Not Know Myself," "Light of the World," "Palms and Hands," "Recompense," and "*Vexilla Regis Prodeunt Inferni*"

Poetry After 9-11: An Anthology of New York Poets: "New York"

Poetry New York: "A to Z," "Coney Island," and "Father Dreams"

Shade: "For C.," "For Harvey Shapiro," "For M. Ziesk," "High School," and "Joan"

Shofar: "I Could Not Say"

St. Luke's Review: "Religious"

The Bad Henry Review: "Seasonal"

The KGB Bar Book of Poems: "Gail"

The New Yorker: "Macy's Elegy" and "Rapunzel: Starbucks"

The Paris Review: "For Michael Heller"

The Southern California Anthology: "Autobiography" and "The Street Light"

The St. Ann's Review: "12 Views of Freetown, 1 View of Bumbuna" and "2001"

The Virginia Quarterly Review: "Case History: Melencholia," "On the Other Side of the Poem," and "The *Daily Racing Form*"

To Stanley Kunitz, With Love: "Somebody Stand Up and Sing"

Thanks, too, to *The Best American Poetry* 2002 for reprinting "I Do Not Know Myself."

The author also thanks Roberta Allen, Beth Bosworth, Janet Coleman, Maggie Paley, Elizabeth Macklin, Harvey Shapiro, and Susan Wheeler for their input to particular poems.

A 2003 grant from the New York Foundation for the Arts (NYFA), which the author gratefully cites, bought time for work on several poems.

And special thanks to Susan Braudy for her friendship and close reading.

photo by Jayne Holsinger

Hugh Seidman was born in Brooklyn (NY). His books have won
several awards including: the Green Rose Prize (*Somebody Stand Up
and Sing*), the Yale Younger Poets Prize (*Collecting Evidence*), and the
Camden Poetry Award (*People Live, They Have Lives*). His *Selected
Poems: 1965-1995* received a Critics' Choice "Best Books" citation and
was listed as one of the "25 Favorite Books of 1995" by The Village
Voice. He has also won three New York State poetry grants (NYFA
and CAPS) and three National Endowment for the Arts (NEA)
fellowships. Seidman has taught writing at the University of Wisconsin,
Yale University, Columbia University, the College of William and Mary,
and the New School University—among other institutions.

New Issues Poetry & Prose

Editor, Herbert Scott

Vito Aiuto, *Self-Portrait as Jerry Quarry*
James Armstrong, *Monument in a Summer Hat*
Claire Bateman, *Clumsy*
Maria Beig, *Hermine: An Animal Life* (fiction)
Michael Burkard, *Pennsylvania Collection Agency*
Christopher Bursk, *Ovid at Fifteen*
Anthony Butts, *Fifth Season*
Anthony Butts, *Little Low Heaven*
Kevin Cantwell, *Something Black in the Green Part of Your Eye*
Gladys Cardiff, *A Bare Unpainted Table*
Kevin Clark, *In the Evening of No Warning*
Cynie Cory, *American Girl*
Jim Daniels, *Night with Drive-By Shooting Stars*
Joseph Featherstone, *Brace's Cove*
Lisa Fishman, *The Deep Heart's Core Is a Suitcase*
Robert Grunst, *The Smallest Bird in North America*
Paul Guest, *The Resurrection of the Body and the Ruin of the World*
Robert Haight, *Emergences and Spinner Falls*
Mark Halperin, *Time as Distance*
Myronn Hardy, *Approaching the Center*
Brian Henry, *Graft*
Edward Haworth Hoeppner, *Rain Through High Windows*
Cynthia Hogue, *Flux*
Christine Hume, *Alaskaphrenia*
Janet Kauffman, *Rot* (fiction)
Josie Kearns, *New Numbers*
Maurice Kilwein Guevara, *Autobiography of So-and-So: Poems in Prose*
Ruth Ellen Kocher, *When the Moon Knows You're Wandering*
Ruth Ellen Kocher, *One Girl Babylon*
Gerry LaFemina, *The Window Facing Winter*
Steve Langan, *Freezing*
Lance Larsen, *Erasable Walls*
David Dodd Lee, *Abrupt Rural*
David Dodd Lee, *Downsides of Fish Culture*
M.L. Liebler, *The Moon a Box*
Deanne Lundin, *The Ginseng Hunter's Notebook*
Barbara Maloutas, *In a Combination of Practices*
Joy Manesiotis, *They Sing to Her Bones*
Sarah Mangold, *Household Mechanics*
Gail Martin, *The Hourglass Heart*
David Marlatt, *A Hog Slaughtering Woman*
Louise Mathias, *Lark Apprentice*